Animals of the Mountains

Élisabeth de Lambilly-Bresson

Gareth Stevens
Publishing

The Brown Bear

I am a brown bear.
In winter, I look for a den.
I am very sleepy then.
The rest of the year,
I eat and eat.
Honey is my favorite treat.

The Marmot

I am a marmot.
Because I am small,
I have to look out!
When an enemy shows up,
I whistle a warning
to my friends.
Then we all run and hide.

The Chamois

I am a chamois.
I spring from rock to rock
like a mountain acrobat.
At play, I run and jump
with ease, then I climb high
where no one sees
my little horns
and striped face.

The Marmot

I am a marmot.
Because I am small,
I have to look out!
When an enemy shows up,
I whistle a warning
to my friends.
Then we all run and hide.

The Eagle

I am an eagle.
I float and glide
across the skies,
hunting with my eagle eyes.
Then I swoop down
to grab my prey
before it can think
of running away.

The Stoat

I am a stoat.
I have a brown coat,
but in winter,
my fur turns white.
I look like a weasel,
I climb like a squirrel,
and I never run from a fight.

The Ibex

I am an ibex.
My sure-footed hooves
make me the king
of mountain climbers.
My long, bumpy horns
help me fight.
They also make
good back-scratchers!

The Wolf

I am a wolf.
I am a great hunter
with a super sense of smell.
I can chase my dinner
until I catch it
because I have strong legs
that are made for running.

Please visit our Web site at: www.garethstevens.com
For a free color catalog describing Gareth Stevens Publishing's
list of high-quality books, call 1-800-542-2595 (USA) or
1-800-387-3178 (Canada). Gareth Stevens Publishing's fax: 1-877-542-2529.

Library of Congress Cataloging-in-Publication Data

Lambilly-Bresson, Elisabeth de.
   [A la montagne. English]
   Animals of the mountains / Elisabeth de Lambilly-Bresson. — North American ed.
      p. cm. — (Animal show and tell)
   ISBN: 978-0-8368-8207-0 (lib. bdg.)
   1. Mountain animals—Juvenile literature. I. Title.
QL113.L3413   2007
591.75'3—dc22   2007002555

This North American edition first published in 2008 by
Gareth Stevens Publishing
A Weekly Reader® Company
1 Reader's Digest Road
Pleasantville, NY 10570-7000 USA

Translation: Gini Holland
Gareth Stevens editor: Gini Holland
Gareth Stevens art direction and design: Tammy West

This edition copyright © 2008 by Gareth Stevens, Inc. Original edition copyright
© 2001 by Mango Jeunesse Press. First published as *Les animinis: À la montagne*
by Mango Jeunesse Press.

Printed in the United States of America

2 3 4 5 6 7 8 9 11 10 09 08